ALL THE WORDS
I KEPT INSIDE

by

By P. J. Gudka

Dearest reader,

My sincerest thanks for reading my book. "All The Words I Kept Inside" is the first book I have ever published. For the last four years, I poured my heart and soul into it. In these poems, I laid bare the deepest and darkest corners of myself. These poems are not always uplifting but they are my truth. These truly are all the words I kept inside for all my life. I'm finally ready to share them.

— P. J. Gudka

All The Words I Kept Inside

All the words I kept inside
In you, I now confide
Today I come to you baring each and every wound in my heart
The memories of every time it's been ripped apart
Keep my heart safe and hold it tight
Please don't let it out of your sight
Or you will lose your voice just like me
And words become the only thing that sets you free

"The paradox of trauma is that it has both the power to destroy and the power to transform and resurrect."

- Peter A. Levine

No One Listens To Me, So I Write

No one listens to me
Even when I yell
So I sit here and write
Because I have a story to tell

Death

It's harder to mourn the dead
When they're still alive

Let Go

Like fire
Ice burns too
When you hold on for too long
It's time to let go
Move on

Stop Running

I spent my whole life running
From my problems
Why did it take me so long to realize
They were running with me

Scars Of The Past

The scars of the past
Make it much easier
To lock up my heart
And throw away the keys
Never letting anyone in
Even when I feel lonely

Compliant In My Own Unraveling

Terrified of everyone
Shaking at the thought
Of fighting for myself
Instead, I cower in my bed
And do as I am told

The Road To Nowhere

I was scared and alone
So I took the road to nowhere
I felt like I was suffocating
So I took the road to nowhere
I felt like I couldn't be myself
So I took the road to nowhere
I felt stuck in a place I hated
So I took the road to nowhere

I thought the road to nowhere would lead me
To a place where I fit in
To a place where I could be myself
To a place where I was happy
But I feel just as lost here as I did back then

To The Child I Was

"You were such a quiet child"
Because no one listened when I spoke

Be Yourself
(But Our Version Of You)

Trying to be myself

In a world that worships uniformity

I am torn between wanting to be accepted

And wanting to be happy

Trying so hard to break free

Of the chains of societal norms

Fighting every day to be me

But still wanting to keep everyone else happy

The Youngest Sibling

Too young to make decisions
Too old to not
Too young to know how the world works
Too old to not
Too young to know what's best
Too old to not

Speak Up

"Speak up," they always told her
"Shut up," they told her when she did

Like A Caged Bird

Like a caged bird, I sit here and sing
Because you went ahead and clipped my wing
In this cage, I forever will stay
For love, a heavy price to pay
I will never truly be free
At least not in the way God intended for me to be

In The Present

Live in the now
And not the past
For what is now yesterday
Was once today

The Sins Of The Living

When I was a child
I was terrified of ghosts
As an adult I'm terrified
Of the living

Scars

The scars on my soul
Now remind me
That the wounds once left there
Have finally healed

A Stagnant Soul

It was not the ups
Or the downs
That broke my soul
It was always the stagnancy
Knowing that this is the rest of my life
That is what I find unbearable

An Old Friend

Once a friend
Later a foe
Now a stranger
I no more know

There Is No Winning

The choices are
To live in the real world
And feel all the pain
I've held in for years
Or live in my dreams
And lose all the happiness
The present has to offer

The Monster Under My Bed

I fell in love
With the monster under my bed
I fell in love
With myself

Inner Child

I weep for my inner child
She didn't stand a chance

The Past Was Once The Present

So preoccupied with what was
That we forget about what is
Until it too becomes what was

Make It Stop

Using me as armor
To protect yourselves
Every day I bleed through these wounds
No amount of bandages
Will ever make it stop

Life Is Cruel

People all around you
When all you want is to be on your own
Nothing but chaos
When all you want is some peace
The older you get
The more life seems like a cruel joke

Boundaries

People want you around
Until you learn to say no
Once your boundaries are found
They can't wait for you to go

Bullets Don't Always Hit
The Right Targets

Anger and spite

Like bile in the mouth

Spewing venom

At everything in sight

Misguided frustrations

Lack of control

Years of trauma

Overflowing

Poison in a cup

That has runneth over

Nothing Is Unconditional

No one to comfort her
Or ask her if she's okay
Cursed to be forever alone
With no one in her corner
Even those who were supposed to love her unconditionally
Abandoned her from the beginning

An Abundance Of Wound

Time does not heal all wounds
It just creates fresher ones
That overshadows your old wounds

Once Upon A Time,
I Was Just Like You

I was not always like this

Surely and cold

Once I too had been young

And full of hope

Warmly smiling at everyone around me

Eyes wide with curiosity

I was just like you

And one day

You will be just like me

A Moment Of Silence
For Who You Once Were

It's okay to mourn the person you were
Even if you love the person you are now

The Fire Inside

Fire burning inside me
Flame growing
With every tear
Falling down my cheek
Holding on to the anger
And the deceit
Fuelling my own fire
While simultaneously
Trying to put myself out

Everything Will Be Okay Tomorrow

Daydreams of a better tomorrow
Get me through today
Daydreams of a better tomorrow
Save me when the present is unbearable
Daydreams of a better tomorrow
That I know will never be real
Daydreams of a better tomorrow
I still believe in
Daydreams of a better tomorrow
Because these daydreams are all I have

"Anxiety is a thin stream of fear trickling through the mind. If encouraged, it cuts a channel into which all other thoughts are drained."

—*Arthur Somers Roche*

Caged

Every day I think
That I am finally free
Only to realize
That my cage
Is simply getting bigger

Maladaptive Daydreaming

My self-made escape
My self-made prison

Her

Her mind is full of flowers
But unable to express her thoughts
She sits silently in the corner
Resigned to be a wallflower

Perfectionist

Always good enough
Never perfect
Always tries her best
Never feeling better than okay

Compliant In My Own Unraveling

Terrified of everyone
Shaking at the thought
Of fighting for myself
Instead, I cower in my bed
And do as I am told

Life And Death

I have never been afraid
To die
I have only ever been afraid
To live

Good Memories

The good memories haunt me
More than the bad ones
It's always
The what ifs
The what could have beens
That occupies my mind
When I'm alone

Surrounded By The Monsters

The monsters were never under my bed
They were always inside my head
And they follow me everywhere I go
Trying to pull me down below

A Flower Cursed To Be Trampled On

I feel trapped
In this box
What is a woman?
How would you describe
A meadow of flowers
Each one more beautiful than the last
Every single color you can imagine
And some you have never seen before
How can you admire
The beauty before your eyes
And cut these flowers
Just to pack them into a box
And seal it tightly
Never allowing anything
But uniformity

My Greatest Enemy

Terrified of being forever alone
Lost in a world of dreams
My only escape from reality
Is my greatest enemy

Chaos All-Around

Chaos all-around
Searching for a sanctuary
None to be found

Hope

Hope is a dangerous succubus
She seduces us all
With her wicked smile
And her shimmering eyes
She extends her hand
Only to pull you down with her
To a fiery fate
You will never escape

A Cage Of My Own Making

Trapped inside a cage
Of my own making
The key rests in my hand
And yet I am unable to use it

Panic Attack

Heart racing

Gasping for air

Hands shaking

Vision blurred

Mind broken

A reflection

Of the soul

Every Day Is A Struggle

Drowning in the anxiety
Inside me
Drowning in the anxiety
That is me
Drowning in the anxiety
I pray to be free

The Flowers In My Mind

Flowers blooming in my mind

Unbeknownst to those around me

Forever in motion

Forced to constantly perform

In this circus

We call life

Words

Haunted by the words I never said
And those I that did say
Words my only friend and my biggest foe

The Heart Of A Writer

Nothing is more fierce than the heart of a writer
Filled to the brim with a million stories untold
Just waiting to burst forth
Like the sunrise after a stormy night.

Always Running But Never Alone

I thought running away would solve all my problems
I did not realize my problems would always run beside me
Like a shadow
They remain, my only companion.

Let Go

Like a crushing weight on my chest
The boulder grows heavier
Every breath feels like the last
My mind is scrambled and unclear
The weight continues to get heavier
Until I can carry it no more
I can no longer be my savior
So I take a deep breath and let go

My World Is On Fire

I thought the world was burning
And everything was on fire
But it was just me
I was the one on fire

There Is No Normal

Desperate for control
In a world out of control
Grasping at any hint of normalcy
Begging for a predictable tomorrow

"People who have never dealt with depression think it's just being sad or being in a bad mood. That's not what depression is for me; it's falling into a state of grayness and numbness."
— Dan Reynolds

The Ramblings Of A Broken Soul

I was not always broken

My eyes not always sunken

Over the years the scars grew

And the happy moments became few

Cracks began to appear

And the joy began to disappear

What was once unadulterated and whole

Became the shattered fragments of a broken soul

Self-Improvement

Every single time I try to make myself better
I end up breaking myself even more
I stitch up one wound
Only for two more to open up
I'm tired of doing this every day
I can't do this anymore

Happy

All she wanted was to be happy
Like everyone else around her
But the older she got
The more she realized
They were all unhappy too

Numb

One for the anxiety
One for the depression
Four pills a day
Keeps the bad thoughts away
For such little pay
You can be numb all-day

Birthdays

Some people hate their birthday
But I love mine
The only thing keeping me alive
Is knowing I'm getting closer to death every year

I Don't Want To Exist Anymore

The older I get
The more my existence
Feels like a burden

I Really Don't Want
To Exist Anymore

"Why do you want to die?"
"Why do you want to keep living?"

I'm Drowning

Deeper into the darkness I fall
Depression's hands waiting to catch me
Further, off the ground, I float
Anxiety's hands waiting to carry me higher

Help Me

Why can no one hear
My cries for help
Every time I smile
I die a little more inside

Painfully Ordinary

I've always felt extraordinary
But I think it's time to admit
I'm just
Painfully ordinary

Tear-Stained Notebooks
On The Shelf

I may have run out of tears
But I never truly stopped crying

Smile

Wake up smiling
Just to cry myself to sleep every night

Feeling Nothing At All Or Everything All The Time

I haven't felt happy in so long
I've forgotten what it feels like

My Imperfect Garden

Happiness so short and fleeting

Never feeling just right

Like a garden

Always one flower

Away from being perfect

Crying For Help

Tears roll down my eyes
I quickly wipe them away
I look around to make sure
No one noticed
A part of me wishes
Someone did

Depression

The pain I feel isn't permanent
The pain I feel isn't rational
The pain I feel has no origin
The pain I feel never goes away

Constant

Why is it that the pain never goes away
But the happiness always fades so quickly

Tired

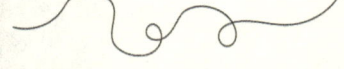

I'm tired of feeling this way
I'm ready for the pain to go away
But I know it's here to stay
At least for another day

Chained To My Demons

Chained to my demons

I drown in pain

Every second I'm conscious

Is a torment in itself

I no longer fear going to hell

Because now I fear

That I'm already in it

One With The Darkness

Drowning deeper in my despair
Darkness my only friend
Light the elusive mistress
I continue to chase after
Even when I know
My place will always be
Beside the darkness
That envelops me

Forever Alone

All alone I walk in this cruel world
Looking for someone's company
But finding none except my own
Cursed to walk this path alone
Life is nothing but a cruel joke

What's Happiness Like?

How nice it must be
To laugh
And actually mean it

Depression, My Distinguished Guest

No longer held down

By your presence

I breathe in the fresh air

Almost as though for the first time

I know someday you will return

But until then

I shall bask in this sun

Enjoying every moment I have

Till darkness once more

Takes over

Just Another Cliche

A suicidal writer
Just another cliche
Shut up and sit down
No one cares what you have to say
No one's listening to the ramblings
Of a soul broken beyond repair

Tears

Tears of joy
Tears of pain
Who decided
They were not
One and the same

I Hate Me Too

Maybe I think everyone hates me
Because I hate me too

Life Always Finds A Way

Nothing ever gets any better
The harder you try to be okay
The worse it gets
And the more life brings you down
When things finally look up
Life finds a way
To bring you to your knees
The pain just never ends

Acceptance

We always think that if we live through the bad parts of life things will eventually get better. Someday we'll make it, someday we'll achieve all our dreams. But what if we don't? What if this is as good as it gets.

"And ever has it been known that love knows not its own depth
until the hour of separation."
– Khalil Gibran

All The Words I Kept Inside

I Miss You

So many people around me
Yet no one compares to your company
I find myself surrounded by people even more
But lonelier than ever before

Happy Endings

I hate happy endings
Because
I know I'll never get one

Good Memories

The good memories haunt me
More than the bad ones
It's always
The what ifs
The what could have been
That occupies my mind
When I'm alone

I Break What I Touch

Don't get too close
Because I might
Break you too

Lover

How can you hurt me so deeply
Without speaking a word
How can I love you so much
When I don't even know you
How can I be this fixated on the idea of you
When I've never even met the real you

Control

I thought you were my knight in shining armor
But you were nothing more than an illusion
I had created to make myself feel in control
When everything was falling apart

My Saviour Is Me

I thought you would come and save me
That you would take away all the pain
Now I know no one is coming
That I'm the only one who can fix me

The Same Kind Of Broken

You are my favorite sin

My perfect mistake

We found true love

In the depths of hell

My Favorite Nightmare

You are my personal Hell
My favorite nightmare
I loathe your touch
And yet I can never get enough
I want to yell "no"
But all I can scream
Is "yes"

I Hate You

In those brief fleeting moments
When you think I don't hate you
And you think that I love you
Just know that I still hate you
In my heart
I have nothing but hate for you

The Right Words

I could never find the right words
To tell you how much I love you
When we were together

But now that you are no longer here
The words just won't stop
Coming to me

Every poem I write
Haunts my soul
Reminding me of what I lost

Haunted

I am not haunted
By the words you said to me
But by the words
You never said
I don't regret the things
I said to you
But rather
The things I never could

Meaningless Apologies

Broken promises

Broken heart

Irreversible damage

Already done

Your apologies mean nothing now

I Break Everything I Love

They say
That the eyes are a mirror
To one's soul
So what do you see
When you look into my eyes
Black as my heart
Don't look for too long
For I fear
They will pull you down too
And together we shall drown
In this dark abyss
For eternity

Alone

Alone in the night
Fluent in silence
Loneliness
My long-time partner
Together forever
Side by side

The Wrong Words At The Wrong Time

A million words

Floating in my mind

But when it comes to you

Only the wrong ones

Seem to reach my mouth

My Ugly

I don't want you to love me for my beauty
I don't want you to love me for my charms
I want you to love me for my ugly
I want you to love me for my darkness
Hold me when I can no longer stand
Hold me when I fall again and again

Acknowledgments

Firstly, I want to thank my parents and sister without whom this book and none of my achievements in life thus far would have been possible. Thank you.

I want to thank Priya, one of the most important people in my life. You have stuck by me all this time, through the good and the bad. I can't even put into words (you would think as a writer I would be better at that) how thankful I am for you. We started out as friends but you're family now (yup, you're stuck with me). You have to be one of the most intelligent, kind-hearted, beautiful, and selfless people I have ever met. I am forever in awe of you. Without your unyielding support and faith in my writing, this book would not exist. Thank you, from the bottom of my heart.

Shreya, from the moment we met, I knew we would become great friends and I was not wrong. You are one of the kindest and sweetest souls I have met. Thank you for the conversations that I will always cherish and I look forward to having many more. You are amazing.

I know we haven't been in the same country in years but thank you, Leah, for always keeping in touch. You will always be one of my closest friends and one of the most brilliant, beautiful, and hardworking people I know.

Tiani, I am so glad our paths crossed. You are an inspiration to me and those around you. The way you have persevered through everything never fails to amaze and motivate me. You are someone I can truly be myself around. Thank you so much for all the support you have shown me.

Yash and Veer, we are family by blood but friends by choice. You two have grown up to be excellent young men with so much potential. Don't ever let anyone dim your light. Thank you for the much-needed breaks from writing and the wonderful memories. I look forward to having many more amazing experiences together.

Thank you to my therapist, Dr. Rechael Mbugwa for her continued support and help. You have helped me get back up at my worst and for that I am so grateful.

I want to thank everyone that has supported my writing on my blog, Lifesfinewhine. My WordPress family, as I like to call them. Thank you so much. Without you, this book would literally not exist. I want to thank Cindy for her constant help, wisdom, and support. I also want to thank Devang for cheering me on every step of the way. Hilary, Jude, Rita, John, Cheryl, Brian, Opher, Destiny, Vanya, Tangie, La'Brea, Joseph, Christopher, Rochelle, Narisa, Janice, Belladonna, Kiki, Steve, Ian, Milena, Sadje, Ranjana, Manoj, Pennie, Lauren and everyone else from WordPress. I'm so sorry if I missed any names but just know that you mean the world to me. Thank you to my Lifesfinewhin-ers, you are the reason I get to live my dream.

Forever grateful,
Pooja

About P.J. GUDKA

P. J. Gudka is a writer, blogger and freelancer currently working from Kenya. Her journey as a blogger began when she created her multi-niche blog, Lifesfinewhine, as a teenager, to share her experiences with life, mental health, travel and more. Since then, her blog has captured the interest of thousands of people around the world and is now her full-time passion. Her writing has been published in books like Hidden In Childhood: A Poetry Anthology and Glow: Self-Care Poetry For The Soul as well as multiple magazines.

What is your truth? What is your secret? What secrets are you keeping from the world that you hope one day you will be brave enough to tell? When will you tell your heart? All The Words I Kept Inside allows you this moment.

This collection of poetry urges you to look deeply inside and confront your darkest thoughts. It takes that inner dread, disappointment, and heartache to reveal the words of the heart. This book will show you that you are not alone. That you are understood. That you don't have to go through these dark moments on your own because so many of us experience them too. The words found inside will reach out a hand and guide you.

This is your moment.

This is your truth that you've never told anyone.

The words see you.

From the very earliest moments, the words know...

"All the words I kept inside
In you, I now confide..."

ISBN 978-1-958531-65-5
90000
9 781958 531655